'This wasn't in the Textbooks': Life as a student nurse

You think you know what it takes to be a student nurse? Think again!

Published by: Demie Risby

Table of contents:

Chapter 1: The Morning After – A Student Nurse's Daily Commute

Ah, the early mornings. They've become a rite of passage in the life of a student nurse, a time when you're neither fully awake nor fully asleep, somewhere between the heavy haze of exhaustion and the fragile alertness only caffeine can provide. You've just worked an all-nighter. No sleep. Not a single second of rest. Your body hums with the after-effects of the night shift—the fluorescent lights that never dim, the endless rounds, the patients who need more than you could give, and yet, somehow, you gave everything you had.

But now, here you are, stepping out into the cold, damp morning. It's almost like the world offers a brief, fleeting moment of calm, but you're too disoriented to appreciate it truly. The world around you feels distant—like a faint echo of the life you've just left behind in the hospital. As the 9-to-5ers shuffle past you, there's an odd disconnect. They're caught in their bubble, staring blankly ahead, unaware of the world you've just inhabited. They have no idea what it's like to have barely blinked all night, to have watched over patients whose stories you'll never fully know, to have been there for them in those quiet, desperate moments that never make the headlines. They have no idea that you are walking through this new day with no sleep, your muscles aching, the exhaustion in your bones, and yet, there's no time to stop. No time to rest.

And then, there's the longing. The deep, desperate need to sit down, to let your body rest just for a moment. But you can't. Not yet. You carry that ache with you like a weight. You're in a bubble—living in a world that only a few can truly understand, where the clock ticks differently and the pace of life moves in strange, unpredictable rhythms. You can almost hear the hum of the hospital still in your ears, the soft beeping of machines, the distant murmurs of voices, the constant buzz of activity. It feels like you've just stepped out of one universe and into another. The people around you—walking past in their suits and ties- are living in a completely different reality.

In that brief moment, you wonder: Do they understand that the world they're walking into is so much more predictable, more structured than the world you've just navigated? You wonder if they understand that, for you, this early morning is merely the aftermath of another life—one where the days are long, the nights even longer, and the exhaustion never truly ends. It's a life where the most mundane of tasks can carry incredible weight, and the fleeting moments of rest are like treasures you can't always claim.

Yet, despite it all, there's something inside of you that refuses to give in to the weariness. Despite the relentless pace, despite the lack of sleep, and despite everything your body aches to tell you, there's still a sense of fulfilment that lingers. You've just been through something few others could understand, and somehow, that makes it worth it.

And it's not just a personal journey, either. A statistic I came across recently indicates that more than 50% of student nurses in the UK report feeling overwhelmed by the demands of their training (Royal College of Nursing, 2024). And you can see why—between early starts, night shifts, endless studying, and the emotional toll of caring for patients, it's a wonder any of us make it through without turning into walking zombies. But despite those staggering numbers, we're still here. We keep going. Because for all the exhaustion and stress, there's something about this work that pulls us forward. It's hard to explain, but it's there, driving us, keeping us from hitting pause.

So, as you ride the underground, train, bus or even walk, and you are surrounded by the sea of faces—some exhausted, some indifferent, some simply lost in their thoughts—you know one thing: You're not one of them. Not really. They don't know what it's like to live in the world you've just stepped out of, and you have no choice but to keep moving through it, carrying that quiet, profound sense of purpose. It may be a rough road ahead, but for now, you have a small window of time to breathe, to exist between worlds. A world that few can understand but all must endure.

And so, the journey continues. One shift at a time, one day at a time. For now, you carry on, grateful for the moments of clarity, even if they're fleeting—because the reality of being a student nurse is a strange one. It's chaotic, exhausting, beautiful, and frustrating all at once. But above all, it's a story you wouldn't change for anything. Because even in the hardest moments, even in the darkest hours, there's always something to learn, something to gain.

Chapter 2: The Unlikely Medley of Student Nurses

Entering the lecture hall feels like stepping into a mini-United Nations of future healthcare professionals. Seriously, you couldn't find a more diverse group if you tried. We've got people from all walks of life, united by one very peculiar choice: to spend our days getting yelled at by patients who have no idea where they are, work 12-hour shifts, and develop an odd fondness for bodily fluids.

First up, we have the fresh-faced teens just out of A-levels. They've barely had time to adjust to the idea of adulting, yet they're already here, armed with enthusiasm and an alarming number of MacBooks. These individuals are ready to take over the world—starting with meticulous notetaking and the ability to organise their coursework as if preparing for a space mission. Sure, they might think that typing 100 words per minute will automatically turn them into experts in blood pressure management, but they are eager to learn and are already off to a good start. Perhaps it's that raw enthusiasm that will make them exceptional nurses in the end, even if they still refer to Crocs as 'sensible shoes.'

Then, there's the crowd who've been around the block a bit. These are the students who decided that whatever they were doing before—be it working in retail, finance, or perhaps even as a professional juggler (honestly, we can't be sure)—wasn't quite fulfilling enough. These are the ones who've seen the world beyond textbooks and are now diving headfirst into the world of bandages and bedpans. They may have handled spreadsheets or pitch meetings with clients, but now they're tackling vital signs and patient care plans. Their confidence is impressive—they've been to the 'real world' and survived-though you'll still catch them wondering if 'business casual' will fly for a clinical placement. (Spoiler: it won't.) But we admire their resilience—starting a whole new career requires a level of grit we can't help but respect.

Then there are the superheroes, a.k.a. the 'mums' (and dads, but let's be real, the mums deserve their own chapter). These are the folks who manage to juggle nursing school, and family life, and still somehow look like they've got it all together. They've been up since 4 a.m., packed lunches, fought with toddlers over shoes, and somehow managed to show up to class with their textbooks in hand and a smile that says, "I've got this"—when, in reality, we all know they're running on nothing but coffee and sheer willpower. If there were a medal for multitasking, they'd win gold, silver, and bronze. They've mastered the art of doing a load of laundry, planning a meal, and still finding time to help classmates with group work. And yes, their mornings may sound like the plot of an action movie, but we're convinced they've got secret ninja skills.

Despite our differences, we form this wonderfully dysfunctional family of nursing students. We're all here for different reasons, with different stories to tell. Some of us are just getting started, some of us are reinventing ourselves, and others are already masters at wearing multiple hats. But the beauty of it is that we're all in it together, facing the same challenges, and learning from one another along the way.

What unites us isn't just the endless assignments or the gruelling clinical placements (though that does help) but rather the fact that we've all chosen, in one way or another, to enter a profession that's tough, rewarding, and, yes, sometimes a bit gross. From the late-night study sessions to the sweaty shifts, we might be exhausted, but we're all here because we're driven by something more. Whether it's that spark of hope that we can make a difference or the knowledge that we're helping people when they're at their most vulnerable, there's a reason we're all sticking with it.

We may all complain about the lack of sleep, the mountains of coursework, or the unending stream of bodily fluids we seem to encounter, but deep down, we know that we wouldn't want to be anywhere else. Because, at the end of the day, there's no greater reward than the feeling that, even if you're covered in vomit, you've made a difference in someone's life.

Chapter 3: The Big Decision - A Memory That Guides Us

You'd think a decision to go into nursing would happen in the logical stages of adulthood, right? Not for me. My journey began at the ripe old age of 6. While most kids were running around playing with their toys, I was learning a whole different set of life skills. You see, when you get diagnosed with a rare form of childhood cancer at such a young age, life changes.

For two long years, I was surrounded by the most incredible people—nurses. Not just any nurses, mind you. These were the warriors who fought for kids like me, who gave everything to make sure I had a fighting chance. They made hospital beds feel like home, they knew just when to crack a joke to ease my mom's nerves, and most importantly, they showed me what it meant to give up everything—time, comfort, family—just to care for someone else.

I could never have imagined, at that tender age, that I'd be standing where I am today. But those nurses were my heroes. Their care, dedication, and empathy didn't just save my life; they shaped who I am. And so, here I am, years later, taking the same journey, hoping to become someone's hero too.

This path isn't unique to me. For many, the decision to enter nursing is a reflection of deeply personal experiences that ignite a passion for caregiving. Take Sarah, a nurse I met during clinical placements. She entered the profession after caring for her grandmother, who was diagnosed with Alzheimer's. The long nights spent making sure her grandmother was comfortable, the heartbreaking moments of watching her memory fade—those were the moments that crystallised Sarah's purpose. It wasn't just about nursing as a career; it was about giving someone the dignity and compassion they deserve at the end of their life. Sarah's story is one of countless others who were moved by the experiences of their own families, leading them to nursing as a way of continuing that love and care for others.

Then there's Harry, who chose nursing after spending time volunteering in a hospital as a teenager. His experiences in the paediatric ward—where he comforted children undergoing chemotherapy—showed him the impact one person could have. Harry's connection with those kids wasn't just about treating their symptoms; it was about being a source of light during some of their darkest moments. For him, nursing became more than a job—it became a commitment to be present, to be kind, and to fight for others in deeply meaningful ways.

His story reminded me that nursing isn't just about medical expertise; it's about building trust and offering emotional support that can sometimes mean just as much as the physical care we give.

Stories like Sarah's and Harry's remind me that the decision to pursue nursing often comes from personal experiences, too—whether it's a family member's illness, a volunteer experience, or a deep-seated desire to offer care and compassion to those in need. It's a journey rooted in both the science of healing and the art of human connection. For many of us, like those nurses who took care of me, it's a path that leads us back to the lessons learned in our moments of vulnerability and strength.

And just like those nurses who shaped my childhood, I hope to carry that same legacy forward. Although, if I'm being honest, I'd settle for at least being able to look confident while taking a patient's blood pressure without panicking that I've put the cuff on backwards. Baby steps.

Chapter 4: Navigating Expectations - The Family Dynamic of a Student Nurse

Family gatherings—those familiar spaces where everyone comes together, shares stories, and celebrates milestones. For most, they are a time of laughter, connection, and reflection. But for a student nurse, they can often be a bit more complicated. Often, we are the first in our generation to pursue higher education, and those gatherings can hold a different weight. While most relatives beam with pride, there's also a gap in understanding that can linger between you. Conversations often revolve around "When will you be done?" or "Are you enjoying it?" but the deeper complexities of being a student nurse go unnoticed. And, well, let's not forget the usual 'I have a rash, can you check', or the 'Your Nan's got this...'. Almost as if one placement in a children's day surgery ward qualifies you as a self-diagnosed medical genius. Often, a simple 'go to the doctor' sorts these out.

At family reunions, I was often asked to explain what being a nursing student entails, and I struggled to put it into words. For them, nursing might be as simple as seeing a nurse in scrubs with a stethoscope, offering comfort to a patient. But the reality is far more demanding and nuanced. The hours spent in classrooms, the clinical placements, the exhaustion from long shifts—none of that is fully grasped by those who have never walked the path themselves. There are also emotional struggles, like when you have to deal with the death of a patient or witness suffering that you can't fix. You don't just study anatomy and pharmacology; you also learn how to manage your emotions, deal with stress, and support families through the most difficult moments of their lives.

Then, there's the expectation of pursuing a higher education, especially when it's not cheap. While they're proud of your accomplishments, there's also an unspoken pressure to succeed, to pave the way for others in the family to follow suit. Relatives often don't understand the gruelling schedule of a nursing student. They assume you're just "studying" all the time, but in reality, you are out in hospitals, shadowing experienced nurses, managing a full course load, and sometimes, balancing part-time jobs just to make ends meet. It's an overwhelming experience that nobody fully understands unless they've been through it themselves. Family and friends don't always grasp the sacrifices: missing birthday parties, skipping holidays, or the exhaustion that comes from spending 12-hour shifts at the hospital, only to come home and keep studying for exams.

The challenge of being a student nurse isn't just about learning the skills to care for patients—it's about finding the balance between your responsibilities and the people who don't quite understand the demands of the journey. While you are grateful for their support, it's hard to explain that nursing school isn't a traditional college experience. It's an intense, immersive, and often emotionally taxing path. You're not just learning textbook knowledge; you're gaining real-world experience with real patients—some of whom may never make it out of the hospital, and others who will forever change your perspective on life.

I've seen things that no one could prepare me for—the heartbreak of a young child diagnosed with terminal cancer, the confusion in the eyes of an elderly patient who can no longer care for themselves, the quiet strength of a mother and father who stays at their baby's bedside for days on end. These are the experiences that shape a nursing student, and they stay with you long after you leave the hospital. But when I return home to my family, it's difficult to translate these moments. How do you explain the weight of those experiences when the person sitting across from you at dinner simply doesn't know what it's like? How do you make them understand that while you're grateful for their support, your world is full of heavy, life-changing moments that they can't comprehend?

Navigating higher education with nobody to lean on to give you advice often means you have to navigate uncharted waters, not just in the classroom or clinical setting, but in relationships as well. Sometimes, it may feel like you are caught between two worlds—the familiar one of family and friends who want the best for you, and the demanding, intense world of nursing, where the stakes are high, and the learning curve is steep. But what keeps us going is knowing that we are not just earning a degree, we are building a foundation to become the kind of nurses who will make a difference in someone's life.

The road ahead is long no doubt, and yes, there will be more family gatherings where you have to navigate these complicated dynamics. But I also know that my journey, while challenging, shaped me into someone capable of carrying the immense responsibility that comes with being a nurse. It's a path that may be hard for the family to fully understand, but it's one you should all be proud to walk.

Chapter 5: The Basics, the Blood Pressure Cuff, and Everything In Between

You know how when you start nursing school, you're bombarded with all the advanced clinical skills they expect you to master? It's like, "Welcome to the world of healthcare, now here's how to manage an arterial line in intensive care." Wait—what? I've barely figured out how to properly use a blood pressure cuff! Seriously, they'll throw you into the deep end without a life jacket and then ask you to swim across the Atlantic.

I'll admit it—my first day on the ward, I was so nervous I could barely tie my shoes, let alone know how to work a stethoscope, although let's be real do you really want to put those things in your ears after they have done a round through every worker on shift. But the real kicker came when I had to take a patient's blood pressure. You would think a simple task like that would be easy, right? But no. I somehow managed to put the cuff on wrong, and instead of hearing a normal rhythm, all I got was a delightful silence that made me look like a total rookie. I checked the cuff, checked the machine, and checked my pulse to make sure *I* wasn't in some sort of time warp. Eventually, I realised I had the cuff on so high up the arm that I probably could've measured the pressure in their shoulder instead of their forearm. Needless to say, the nurse who was shadowing me had a good laugh at my expense—and gave me a nice lesson about how to actually use the cuff properly.

But it's not just the basic stuff that gets overlooked—it's the weird stuff. You know, the kind of basic things that no one thinks to teach you, like how to change a nappy. Let's be honest—this is a skill most new parents somehow figure out in the first 48 hours of life with their newborns, but me? Well, as a student nurse, I had all the fancy tricks for inserting IVs, managing ventilators, and handling arterial lines, but when it came to changing nappies, I was looking at it like it was some sort of puzzle with several of the pieces missing. I just stared at the nappy, unsure whether to pull, twist, or maybe call in backup.

And don't get me started on the lines—arterial lines, central lines, PICC lines, the works. I could tell you exactly which way to turn the 3-way tap to draw blood from the arterial line. But ask me how to help a new parent change their baby's nappy for the first time, and I'll look at you like you just asked me to perform brain surgery. It's funny how they expect us to know the *advanced* stuff without ever asking, "Hey, do you know what BP means or even to fix a bed without making it look like a tornado just passed through?"

And this is where the lines between doctors and nurses start to get blurry. Suddenly, we're expected to know how to handle the same level of advanced equipment as the doctors, but with fewer years of schooling (and zero practical training on the little stuff). Sure, we're taught how to handle the tech, but somehow no one ever thinks, "Maybe they'll need to know how to fold a hospital gown properly, too." It's almost like there's a hidden curriculum that says, "Forget about the basics. Here's a crash course in advanced clinical care. Oh, and here's a video on 'How to Deal with Overwhelming Stress and Laugh It Off in Public' yeah, right!

Honestly, I sometimes wonder if they assume we came into nursing school with a basic understanding of everything like we've all had some secret, pre-programmed knowledge downloaded into us before stepping onto the ward. The only thing I was sure about was that I was going to get a lot of things wrong. But the reality is: no one tells you about these gaps. They teach you advanced stuff that doctors sometimes don't even know, yet they forget to teach you fundamental things- like how to help a confused patient with dementia find their glasses or how to navigate the weird maze of hospital policies that seem to change every two hours and differ by each NHS trust, further confusing each nurse that dares step a foot from one hospital to another. You think using your mate's shower is hard? Try stepping into a new hospital unit, sometimes 3 times a year and being told a dozen different ways of setting up the same IV tray.

One day, I'll glide through a shift like I've been doing this for years—confident, efficient, and totally in control. I'll know exactly where everything is, and how to handle every machine, and I won't need to triple-check my notes before answering a question. But today? Today, I'm just hoping I don't accidentally press the emergency alarm instead of the call bell, that I don't mix up saline with sterile water (again), and that I can make it through one simple procedure without looking like a colour-blind person trying to defuse a bomb. Nursing school teaches you a lot, but nothing quite prepares you for the daily chaos of real-life practice. So for now, I'll keep faking confidence, nodding along like I completely understand the 15 new abbreviations I just heard, and hoping that by some miracle, I make it through the shift without becoming the latest 'learning experience' for the team.

Chapter 6: The Future of Nursing – What's Next? (Spoiler: It's a Bit of a Mess)

So, what's the future of nursing looking like? Well, if I'm being truthful, it's kind of like trying to predict the weather in Britain—one minute it's sunny, the next it's pouring with rain, and before you know it, there's a snowstorm. The truth is, that nursing is evolving, and while there are some exciting changes ahead, there's also a bit of a storm brewing that no one talks about. Except, of course, when you're out on the picket line holding a protest sign, wondering how we went from people clapping on their doorsteps for the NHS to fighting just to be paid a decent wage.

First off, let's talk about the blurred lines between junior doctors and nurses. And I'm not referring to the fact that significantly more men are entering nursing than before. No, I mean the reality that nowadays, the roles of nurses and doctors are becoming a little bit… let's say, 'fuzzy.' In theory, doctors and nurses are meant to complement each other—doctors diagnose, nurses care. Simple, right? But lately, it seems like nurses are expected to take on more responsibility than ever. We're managing critical patients, adjusting medications, interpreting lab results, and (oh, don't forget!) trying to keep everyone's spirits up while we all run around like headless chickens.

I mean, I don't want to throw shade on the hardworking doctors (they've got their mess to sort out), but sometimes it feels like we've crossed a line into a strange grey area where everyone is expected to do everything. And frankly, it's hard to keep up. We're doing more advanced tasks while still trying to figure out how to change a nappy. The distinction between 'junior doctor' and 'nurse' has become so thin, that you'd need a magnifying glass to spot it. We're expected to be expert care providers and critical thinkers, all while still having to pick up the pieces when someone forgets the basics.

But here's the kicker—student nurses in the UK are facing even more challenges. In fact, the number of student nurses has been on the decline for the past few years. According to the latest stats, there are now fewer student nurses than ever before, which is a bit of a crisis. Between 2020 and 2023, the number of students accepted onto nursing courses in England decreased across all regions, sometimes up to a 40% decline. (Royal College of Nursing, 2024). Now, I don't know about you, but if we're supposed to be tackling a growing healthcare crisis with fewer and fewer nurses, it's starting to feel a little bit like trying to solve a jigsaw puzzle with half the pieces missing. It's no wonder we're all a bit frazzled.

But wait, there's a silver lining—well, sort of. The government has reintroduced the nursing bursary in an attempt to get more people into the profession. It's like throwing a lifeline to a sinking ship, but you can't help but wonder: Will it be enough? The bursary is a great initiative, but there's still a huge uphill battle when it comes to attracting people to a profession that is already under strain. And here's where it gets even trickier: the nurses who qualified after COVID have been through a completely different training experience. They spent much of their time in classrooms rather than on the wards, which means they missed out on a huge chunk of hands-on experience.

Picture this: You've spent years studying, and attending countless Zoom lectures (thankfully, in pyjamas), but when it's time for your clinical placements…it's all a bit of a mess. Some nurses qualified with little to no time on the wards, and that gap in training may be starting to show. The post-COVID batch of nurses may have been given the theoretical knowledge, but the practical skills, unfortunately, took a hit. And don't even get me started on the emotional toll—many of these nurses entered the workforce during one of the most chaotic periods in healthcare history, with patients piling up and morale at rock bottom.

Imagine walking into your first day as a nurse and being expected to handle a crisis of this magnitude without ever having the proper exposure. That's a lot of pressure. You approach your mentor, bright-eyed, passionate, and ready to learn those essential skills. They look you in the eye with a piercing glare, thinking, 'Why are you so chirpy?' and then send you off to restock the cupboards or slap a 3M facial mask on you and send you off to help the poor nurse who is run off their feet and in the infectious cubicle alone.

But perhaps those nurses have a story to share- one they can barely comprehend themselves, let alone share as a learning opportunity. It's a story of pain, suffering, and endless days spent in PPE that make them want to throw up. Oh, and faint too, because they couldn't sip a single drop of water without needing to de-gown as if returning from space. I mean, how do you tell an eager new student that you spent hundreds of hours caring for people who suffered right in front of you? Not quite the vibe they're looking for on the first day, that's for sure.

But the bottom line is: Despite all the challenges, we still soldier on. The nursing profession isn't just about what we know, but how we adapt. We've always been flexible, resilient, and able to think on our feet—and that's what's going to get us through these tricky times. The future of nursing may be a bit uncertain, but if there's one thing we know, it's that nurses are always needed. It's just a matter of whether we'll have enough of us to go around.

So, what does this mean for the future of care? Well, nurses will likely continue to be asked to do more with less, and the lines between doctor and nurse will keep blurring. But if you ask me, that just means we'll have to sharpen our skills even more. And hey, if we can manage to tackle the big stuff—arterial lines, ventilators, and all that jazz—maybe, just maybe, we'll get a refresher course on how to properly change a nappy, too.

After all, we're not just here to save lives. We're here to keep things running, pick up the slack, and somehow keep a smile on our faces while we're at it. And when the world expects us to do more with less, we'll just keep on doing what we do best—being the unsung heroes of healthcare, one blurred line at a time.

Chapter 7: Shift Change – The Great "Will I Get to Go Home Early?" Gamble

Ah, shift change—the most thrilling part of any nursing day. It's like the final round of a game show, where the grand prize is either the privilege of going home on time or the unfortunate burden of staying late for the handover. The stakes? Your sanity. The outcome? Entirely dependent on who you're working with that day. The question I have come to dread is always the same: 'Will they let me go home early, or will I have to hand-over?' I don't know why I always hope for the former, and you will too, but you will also be considering deep down that it's like wishing for a unicorn to gallop through the ward. But still, there's that tiny glimmer of hope. Will today be my lucky day?

Now, let's be clear—this isn't some grand decision that is made based on your actual workload or your contributions, no, no. This is purely people-dependent. It's the luck of the draw, like flipping a coin, except the coin has a scowl on one side and an 'I can't be bothered with handover' on the other. If you're lucky enough to get the latter, you'll get the coveted "Yeah, go ahead, you've done enough" from the senior nurse. It's basically like hearing the words, "You've won a small fortune" in the form of a few hours of freedom. But, on the flip side, when the nurse you're working with insists that every student nurse has to do the handover, you can feel the daggers of resentment piercing the back of their head. That scowl you give them? Yeah, it's real. It's the only thing keeping you from losing your mind as you prepare for another 30 minutes of endless reporting.

Every shift change has its unspoken rules, and one of them is the great escape. Some slip away unnoticed, blending into the background like ninjas in scrubs, while others make the rookie mistake of lingering too long, only to be handed a task just as they are about to leave. It's a delicate balance—move too fast, and it looks suspicious; hesitate, and you're trapped in the handover vortex. And then there's the ultimate wildcard: the sympathetic nurse who decides to take pity on a student and grant them early release, like some kind of workplace parole officer. It's rare, but when it happens, it feels like winning the lottery. The only difference? The prize isn't money—it's a full hour of uninterrupted freedom and the chance to make it home before collapsing from exhaustion, or at a reasonable time to have dinner for once.

Of course, no one admits to leaving early without a fight. At placement debriefs, the post-shift analysis begins: Who stayed the latest? Who was stuck in a never-ending conversation about a patient's pet? And who, against all odds, made it out in record time? The unspoken rule is clear—if someone managed an early exit, it's best not to rub it in too much. After all, once the student title is gone, so is the last hope of escaping before handover becomes a permanent part of life. For now, it's just another game of luck, strategy, and the occasional well-timed disappearance.

Chapter 8: The Caffeine Crisis – And Other Addictions

Let's talk about addictions, shall we? We're all guilty of a few. For most student nurses, it begins innocently enough with caffeine—just a little sip of the ol' coffee to keep you awake during that 12-hour shift. But it doesn't take long before your body develops a serious relationship with caffeine. It's not a simple "I like coffee," it's more like a "I NEED you, coffee. Don't leave me now, I'm only half a person without you." Your veins may as well be made of espresso by this point, and honestly, if there's no coffee machine in sight, you're pretty sure your whole world is about to collapse.

But caffeine isn't the only thing fuelling us through the daily grind. Oh, no. There's also food, that comforting friend who never lets you down, especially during those all-too-familiar night shifts. There's the classic "snack attack" that kicks in around 3 AM when you're running on fumes, and you find yourself devouring an entire packet of biscuits like you haven't eaten in days. Does the packet of chocolate digestive biscuits solve your problems? Not exactly. But do you feel a little bit better in that moment? You bet you do.

And then there's the alcohol—because you know what, after a 12-hour shift of wiping other people's tears and keeping your sanity intact, a glass of wine seems like the only logical thing to do. Just a little something to wind down after a day of saving lives and getting your hands covered in who-knows-what. A glass of wine (or a bottle with a straw) can become the balm for your tired soul. If a glass of vino isn't going to fix your post-night shift terrors, I don't know what will.

But here's the kicker—we all know the reality of being a nursing student isn't all about those midnight snacks or the 17 cups of coffee a day. Oh no. It's about the expanding waistline, which happens so sneakily that one day, you wake up and realise your uniform feels a little tighter than before. According to research, nearly 50% of student nurses gain weight during their studies (Silva et al., 2019). Surprise! It's not because we suddenly developed a deep love for pizza (although, no judgment there)—it's because we don't have time to eat properly, we grab whatever's quick, and we rely on caffeine and sugar to keep us going. Oh, and those late-night snacks? They're practically a requirement when you're working shifts that turn into a 16-hour day.

But let's be real here—this isn't just about the numbers on the scale. It's about survival. You do what you have to do to get through the day. And if that means chugging a litre of coffee followed by a greasy burger and a quick nap in the staff room, then so be it. We'll deal with the consequences later. Maybe in a few years, when we've finally got our life together and can properly meal prep.

In the meantime, we embrace the chaos and the caffeine and laugh about it with friends who are probably in the same boat. After all, at least we're all in this mess together. It's like a weird, caffeine-fuelled support group, where the only real goal is to survive—and if we gain a little weight along the way, well, at least we have a great story to tell about it.

Chapter 9: The Ward Drama – The Heartbreaking and Heroic Moments Behind the Scrubs

Behind every patient's bed is a story—a drama, a mystery, a comedy. And we student nurses? We're the front-row audience to it all. Sometimes, it feels like we should start taking notes for a soap opera that's destined for daytime television (basically boring television for old people). Seriously, if there was a camera following us around, I'm convinced we could give *Grey's Anatomy* a run for its money.

There's always the patient who insists on being "the one" who makes your life difficult. You know the type—the ones who press the buzzer every five minutes because they've somehow become convinced that their every need is of the utmost importance. "I can't breathe!" they'll say after you've just adjusted their pillow for the fiftieth time. Of course, you know they're fine; they just need a little attention. You've got to admire their dedication to dramatic flair. It's as if they've rehearsed their role for years, and now they're ready for their big performance.

But then, there are the ones who are oddly too calm. They've got that "I've been here, done this, got the T-shirt" vibe, even though you're still trying to figure out how to adjust the bed properly. Picture the elderly gentleman who's been in and out of the hospital more times than you can count, yet greets each new nurse with the same warm smile and a 'How are you, love?' He's got a medical history longer than the Harry Potter book series, and half of it feels like it should be in a museum, but somehow, he's always got a joke at the ready. He knows exactly what he needs before you do, and he's the one who'll give you advice about life as if he's been through it all and emerged with wisdom that'll make your future less terrifying.

And of course, there's the never-ending drama that comes with the 'do not resuscitate' conversations. They're never easy, are they? As a student, you're asked to sit in on these discussions, doing your best to keep your professional face intact while inside, your heart is breaking. You're trying to talk calmly, but your hands are shaking. You're trying to respect the family's wishes, yet you can't help but feel the weight of what you're asking—of what it all means. These are the moments that stay with you long after your shift ends, the ones you think about when you're lying awake in bed at night, trying to process the gravity of it all.

But the reality is—*this* is the side of nursing that no one tells you about. These tough moments, the ones that rip at your heartstrings, teach you the most. You're expected to handle them with grace, professionalism, and a brave face. But inside, you're a mess. You're learning how to manage the unexpected, how to communicate under pressure, and, perhaps most importantly, how to laugh when it feels like the world is collapsing around you. If you can survive the ward drama, especially the tough conversations about life, death, and everything in between—you can survive anything.

Then there are the days when you walk into a room filled with medical professionals and the parents of a critically-ill child. And for a second, you forget to breathe. You know you have to be strong. You know you have to say or listen to the words that no parent ever wants to hear, but at that moment, it's hard to do it without your voice shaking. You're asked to sit in a room as a student barely out of the classroom and listen as the consultant delivers test results that are anything but good; results that suggest a bleak outcome. And no matter how prepared you think you are, no matter how many textbooks you've read, there's nothing that quite prepares you for the weight of those moments.

You must put on a brave face. You must hold it together, not just for the parents who are hanging on to your every word, but also for the child who is lying there, fighting for their life. You try to be compassionate, to be there for the parents, to offer support, but inside, you're shaking. Because no matter how much you train, no matter how much you prepare, you still can't take away the heartache of losing a child.

Often in nursing, in the middle of that heartbreak, there's a moment of connection. There's that thank you, that small act of kindness, the moment when a parent places a small box of chocolates in your hand as a token of appreciation. In that moment, you're reminded why you're doing this job, why all the struggles and the tears are worth it. You might be holding back your own tears, but their gratitude feels like a balm on your tired soul.

And then, there are the moments when you have to be present during the most gut-wrenching experience of all—the resuscitation of a newborn baby. You're standing there, part of a team, trying to save a tiny life. You hear the alarms going off, and the rush of voices as everyone works in a coordinated frenzy. And you're there, right in the thick of it, doing your part—whether it's handing tools, watching the clock, or being thrown hands-first into CPR. The room is filled with tension, blood, and the weight of what's at stake. You try not to look too closely at the life-or-death situation unfolding, but you can't help but notice the tiny hands, the fragile heartbeat, and the hope hanging in the balance. And when that baby finally takes a breath, when the tension breaks and you hear a faint cry, there's a moment of pure relief—like a tiny miracle unfolding right before your eyes.

But be prepared for the moments when this little soul does not take a breath; trust me, the time will come. And know this: it is a truly heart-wrenching and painful moment. Remember, everyone around you feels the same way—you are all in this together, and this will help guide you through. It's these experiences that stay with you long after you've clocked out, long after the day has ended. They are what make the long shifts, the missed meals, and the exhaustion that much more difficult. But, you must remember, at the end of the day, you realise that being part of someone's most vulnerable moments, whether it's their heartbreak or their miracle, is what makes this job so incredibly meaningful.

Nursing is full of these moments—the highs, the heartbreaks, the absolute absurdities. And as I walk off the ward at the end of another emotionally exhausting shift, I think: If this was an episode of *Grey's Anatomy*, at least I'd have dramatic background music to make it feel more cinematic. Instead, I just have the sound of my own stomach growling. Typical.

Chapter 10: The Great Supply Mystery – Pocket-Sized Pharmacy, Missing Shoes, and the Hunt for Food

Ah, supplies. They say the key to a successful shift is having everything you need, right? Well, in the NHS, that could be described as wishful thinking. It's more like the "Great Supply Mystery"—and as a student nurse, you're often the one who embarks on the quest to find whatever is missing. You need gloves? Sorry, that's "out of stock." You need a syringe? Well, you're likely to find one, but it may have wandered off to a completely different department by the time you need it. And don't even get me started on water. Now you might be thinking, but water? Is this not a basic human right? Well, yes, but enter NHS staff rooms, where you either have to rely on bottled water that only comes along if you beg for it or a poorly-fitted 'filter tap' that breaks quicker than it takes to fix it. But no fear, if you're feeling especially brave that day, the tap will of course do, that is if you choose to ignore the big red sign above it stating that it is not drinkable due to a pseudomonas outbreak. That's just the reality of life in the NHS. Where the patients are sick and, well, so are the staff.

Now, speaking of pockets—let's talk about them, shall we? Somehow, at the end of every shift, you always seem to have a collection of random supplies you didn't realise you'd swiped. You start your shift with an empty pocket, but by the time you clock out, you're a walking pharmacy. Needles? Check. A plaster (that definitely wasn't yours)? Check. A half-used roll of tape? You bet. Oh, and don't forget the saline solution packets you accidentally 'borrowed' while trying to restock your tray. But the grand prize? The ET tube packet that mysteriously appeared in your pocket—who knew? And let's not forget, the moment you search in your pocket for your pen, which, as per usual, has exploded and has now covered your hands in blue ink, perfect! I mean, are you even a nurse if you don't have an ink stain spread across your pocket? It's almost an incredibly low-budget and heavily accidental badge of honour.

I like to think of it as my personal survival kit: a needle here, some saline there—just in case. Maybe it's a bit like an unintended treasure hunt, where the treasure is often… not so glamorous. But hey, in the world of student nursing, if you don't snag a few bits of tape or an extra plaster, did you even *really* do your job?

And then there's the mystery of missing shoes in the staff room. You would think the staff room is a safe haven, a place to rest for just a few minutes, but alas, it's the Bermuda Triangle of nursing supplies. Somehow, your shoes—those beloved, hard-worn shoes that have taken you through the trenches of every 12-hour shift—have vanished. You're certain you left them under the chair, but when you come back after a quick break, they're nowhere to be found. So, what's a student nurse to do? You check every corner of the staff room, and then… BAM—there they are, comfortably on the feet of a colleague who swears they're just 'borrowing' them for a quick round. Sure, your shoes may have been 'borrowed,' but it's just as likely you're walking back to the ward in just your socks. Moral of the story? Taking your smelly shoes home after each shift might be the safer bet.

And food—now there's a completely different story. When you're in the NHS, you might think the staff room is where you can refuel after a long shift, but it's more like a disappointment buffet. The cupboards are stocked with cheap white bread and jam, and you think to yourself, *Okay, at least I can make some toast.* If you're feeling posh, you might even squeeze a sachet of instant coffee into your mug, but that's about as thrilling as it gets. Occasionally, you might stumble upon a packet of biscuits—sugary, processed, and just what you need to feel a bit more human again.

But then—just when you think you're destined to live off toast and the occasional sachet of coffee—there's a magical moment. A patient or their family comes in, and they bring donuts. And not just any donuts. Fresh donuts—glazed, fluffy, and as if they were delivered directly from some heavenly bakery (although let's be honest it's usually the leftovers from the hospital shop downstairs). When the smell hits the staff room, it's like a scene out of a movie. Suddenly, you're running over, dodging your colleagues like it's a race. Forget about proper lunch breaks; it's all about those donuts. The donuts become the holy grail, and for the next five minutes, all your worries about supply shortages and long shifts evaporate as you devour that sugary treat like you haven't eaten in days. It's a beautiful moment, one of those rare, fleeting instances where you actually feel like the universe might be giving you a little something back for all the chaos of the day.

Now, when you're not eating white bread or fighting for donuts, you're probably trying to make sense of your latest diet plan. I don't know about you, but every student nurse goes through the phase of trying to *eat better*—until you find yourself face-to-face with the self-proclaimed health guru in the staff room, who's advising you to not eat anything past 6 p.m. Well, that's not ideal, especially when you're gearing up for a night shift and need a meal at 1 a.m. just to stay awake. Suddenly, you feel like you're stuck between a rock and a hard place: do you listen to the 'wellness' expert who probably lives off kale and quinoa, or do you eat that sandwich, knowing it's the only thing keeping you from falling asleep on your feet?

And yet, despite all of this—the missing shoes, the dubious food, and the never-ending search for supplies—the NHS somehow manages to get the job done. Because at the end of the day, it's not about the jam-covered bread or the mystery of who borrowed your shoes. It's about doing the job. It's about the moments when you finally get a thank you when a patient or their family sees your effort and offers a small token of appreciation. It's about the crazy hours, the missing supplies, and the weird conversations you have in the staff room that somehow make you feel like you're not alone in the chaos. Because in the end, it's those little moments—like donuts, or cracking a dark humour joke to get you through your night that will get you through your shift, and your studies - I promise, truthfully: it's all worth it.

Chapter 11: Tears, tantrums and bathroom therapy

Every student nurse will tell you there's an emotional rollercoaster that comes with this job—sometimes you're soaring through the highs of a patient's improvement, and other times you're plummeting into the depths of despair, wondering if you've made a huge mistake by choosing this career.

It's 5 a.m. on a night shift, and you're huddled in the staff toilet, clutching a roll of toilet paper like it's your last hope. You've locked the door because, well, at this point, it's the only place where you can have a bit of privacy. You stare at yourself in the mirror, red-eyed, trying to suppress the wave of tears that have somehow become your constant companion. You wonder how the heck you ended up here, asking yourself, *why didn't I just stick with my dream of becoming a professional napper?* But then you remember the stats—roughly 24% of nursing students don't even make it past their first year (so don't feel bad if you're considering a career change to something less emotionally taxing, like, I don't know, professional cloud-watching) (Siddique, 2018).

For some, the emotional weight is just too much. It's a tough gig, and it's no surprise that so many opt to tap out early. But the bottom line is: if you *did* quit, you wouldn't get to experience those moments that make everything else worth it. Because, let's face it, the NHS is full of chaos. Sometimes it feels like you're running around putting out fires with a teaspoon of water. You're dealing with tired patients, exhausted colleagues, and more paperwork than should legally exist on the planet. But in the midst of all this madness, there are those moments—those ones that stop you dead in your tracks and remind you why you're still going.

It could be something small, like when a patient who hasn't sat up in weeks, suddenly does. You're doing your rounds, feeling like you're just ticking off boxes, and then, out of nowhere, this patient who's been in bed for ages looks up at you with a smile and says, "I did it! I sat up!" And you realise, in that moment, that you've been part of their journey back to health. Or maybe it's the "thank you" from a family member who's so overwhelmed with gratitude that they bring in homemade brownies or a box of chocolates, and suddenly, you feel like you've won a medal—because brownies are the real currency in the NHS.

And let's not forget those emotional conversations. The ones where you're holding a child's hand while they undergo treatment or listening to an elderly patient tell you stories about their life. You try so hard to hold back the tears, but you know what? Some days, it's impossible. And that's okay. You're not made of stone. Sometimes, you need to let the tears come, even if you're in a toilet at 5 a.m. (It's your own private crying room, after all.) But when the tear finally escapes, and you wipe it away, you don't feel weak. You feel human. And maybe, just maybe, you realise that this—the exhaustion, the heartache, the crazy shifts—is exactly where you're meant to be.

But it's not just about the tearful moments. It's also about the laughter that gets you through. For example, the time you and your colleague are emptying a stoma bag (a bag of poo for those lucky enough never to have encountered one) and the accuracy of emptying this bag has been misjudged, resulting in literal human faeces up on you and in your eye. Now you might be wondering what happens if you get somebody's excrement in your eyes. Well, a painful trip to occupational health with a litre of saline wash in your eye. But of course, this is then met with you and your colleagues spending the rest of the shift- and beyond (because they will never let you live this down)- hackling and crying with laughter at the total horror and humour of what has just happened to you. Laughter is your lifeline, because the truth is, if you didn't find humour in the absurdity of it all, you'd probably be locked in the toilet crying every night shift.

And then, of course, there's the one moment that catches you completely off guard: you're having a normal conversation with a parent who's anxious about their child's condition, and suddenly, they thank you for being there. For being the one person who didn't just walk in and out without saying a word, the one who listened, the one who cared. Often these moments can creep up as a student—when you have the opportunity to listen, take these moments, and learn from them, because when you qualify, these are the moments that are harder to recreate. Yes, there is the paperwork, the missing supplies, or the shoes that keep disappearing from the staff room (seriously, where do they go?). It's the fact that, in the smallest, most unexpected ways, you've made a difference. You've connected. You've made someone's life, however brief, just a little bit easier.

But let's be honest: it's hard. There are days when you wonder if it's worth it. When you question why you didn't just become an accountant or a dog walker. There are days when you're holding a newborn baby in your arms, trying to resuscitate them, and all you can think about is how you're not sure you're ready for this level of responsibility. But then the baby takes a breath, or the patient smiles, and you realise that this is why you're doing it. This is what makes you want to keep going, even when the weight of the world feels like it's crushing you.

So yes, there will be moments when everything feels overwhelming, when the exhaustion hits like a freight train, and the only place to process it all is in the nearest bathroom. But then there are the moments that pull you back—the small victories, the unexpected laughs, the patients who remind you why you started this journey in the first place. Maybe it's a heartfelt thank-you, a knowing nod from a senior nurse, or just surviving a shift without spilling bodily fluids on yourself. The bad days will come, but so will the ones that make it all worthwhile. And if all else fails, there's always the sacred ritual of a post-shift snack, where a vending machine chocolate bar somehow tastes like the best meal in the world. Survival comes in many forms.

Chapter 12: The Confidence Act – Or How You Appear to Have It All Together While Still Figuring It Out

If there's one thing that will break your brain as a student nurse, it's the seemingly endless sea of acronyms. "A-E," "EEG," "FBC," "ABG"—and you sit there wondering if these are some secret codes to a spy agency or just the world's least helpful crossword puzzle. Add hospital department lingo into the mix, and suddenly it feels like you've stumbled into a whole new language—one designed to make you feel utterly lost and out of place.

Then there is the magic moment: after some time on the ward, you're sitting through a handover, and then, *bam*, it clicks. You hear "CXR" and know they're talking about a chest X-ray. You know what an "ABG" is (it's not a new cocktail, by the way, it's *Arterial Blood Gas*). Suddenly, you're fluent in this secret medical tongue. You're not just nodding along, hoping someone will explain what a "FBC" means—you're throwing out acronyms like you've been saying them for years. And just when you start to feel like a linguistic genius, a junior student nurse next to you gets that same look of panic you once had, and you realise, *Oh. Right. I was there too.* You smile to yourself, thinking, *I've made it.*

But here's the real kicker: it's not just about knowing the language. There's the whole act of walking into a patient's room with that calm, collected exterior, even though inside you're screaming. You've *got* this, right? But secretly, you're still trying to figure out what goes where and why on earth that particular piece of equipment refuses to cooperate. While the seasoned nurses seem to glide through the day like they've mastered the art of caring for patients with the elegance of a ballet dancer, you're there, fumbling a little with the equipment and praying you don't accidentally startle the patient.

The *confidence act* becomes your best friend—one minute, you're smiling like you know exactly what you're doing, and the next, you're Googling 'How to use a pulse oximeter' in the staff room between rounds. But guess what? No one knows you're internally freaking out. Not even the patients.

(Though sometimes, they might catch on when you're busy trying to remember whether it's 'Left' or 'Right' when you check vital signs.)

Every nurse has been there. You're the one who's supposed to know everything, but inside, it feels like a constant juggling act of trying not to drop the ball. And here's the thing: this *confidence act* is a universal experience. Every nurse, even the ones with years of experience, has moments when they feel like a total imposter. It's like you're constantly juggling patient care, equipment, and everything else while doing your best to look like you've got it all figured out. And it's completely normal to feel like you're balancing on a tightrope, terrified of losing your balance, but doing your best not to show it.

The truth is, the longer you're in nursing, the more you'll realise that you don't need to have everything figured out immediately. Confidence in nursing comes from experience, yes, but it also comes from embracing the fact that you don't always know what's going to happen next. Nursing is a *process*. There's always something to learn, and each shift brings a new challenge or puzzle to solve.

If you're lucky, you'll work under a nurse who genuinely loves to teach. Those who happily explain what they're doing, how they know what they know, and why they've chosen to do things the way they have. Honestly, these nurses are the MVPs. They've learned through their own trial and error, and they want to pass that knowledge on to you, so don't hesitate to ask questions. Because in nursing, we don't just learn from textbooks. We learn from each other's slip-ups, from those "Well, that was embarrassing" moments. But not every nurse is going to be that interested in mentoring you. Some might be too busy, too tired, or simply over students for the day (and that's okay—they're only human).

However, the thing is: even when you feel brushed off or ignored, use it as an opportunity to think about the kind of nurse you want to be. What kind of teacher will you be when it's your turn? What kind of mentor will you be when you're in the position to guide a new student nurse? Reflect on those moments when you're left to figure it out on your own and build your own style of teaching and leadership from them. And trust me, you will get better at it. If there's one thing I've learned, it's that being a great nurse isn't just about knowing the acronyms or being able to listen to lung crackles with ease. It's about constantly evolving, learning, and yes, getting better at pretending that you *totally* know what you're doing.

Now, let's circle back to that stethoscope. That little tool that symbolically shifts you from 'student' to 'nurse,' though the reality is you have no idea what to do with it when it's first handed to you. It's like being given a magic wand with absolutely no idea whether to swish or flick (Potter fans, anyone?). You'll listen to the chest and hear a strange 'whooshing' noise or a 'thump-thump-thump' and think, *Is that normal? Is that me breathing?* You're convinced you've just heard some unholy combination of a heartbeat and a coffee grinder. And don't even get me started on crackles.

Everyone talks about crackles, but when you hear them for the first time, you wonder, *Is that a sign of impending doom, or is it just my nerves acting up?*

And then there's the wheeze. You've read about it and studied the word in your textbooks, but hearing it for the first time through the stethoscope is like hearing a kettle on the brink of explosion. Is it asthma? A severe infection? Or maybe your patient just needs a hot drink? Whatever it is, you're just praying they don't ask you to explain it. And yet, you nod confidently and think, *Yeah, that's a wheeze, alright.* But deep down, you have no idea if it's asthma, pneumonia, or just the sound of your career anxiety.

The truth is, you'll spend a lot of time playing an audio guessing game, hoping you sound professional while secretly wondering if you're the only one who doesn't quite get it. But here's the secret—no one really knows what they're doing at first. Even the seasoned nurses. It takes practice. Eventually, you'll start recognizing the subtle differences between the whooshes, thumps, crackles, and wheezes. But don't expect to master it overnight. Every stethoscope session is another learning opportunity, and each time you listen, you get a little closer to figuring it out.

Confidence in nursing is like a well-placed piece of tape—sometimes it's holding everything together, and sometimes it's barely clinging on. Student nurses learn quickly that half the job is looking calm, while secretly screaming inside. Ask a question, and you risk looking clueless. Stay silent and, suddenly, it's assumed you understand every obscure medical abbreviation thrown your way. There's no in-between. One minute, it's a casual nod during handover; the next, it's a frantic Google search in the staff room, praying no one notices.

But here's the real secret: everyone, at some point, has faked their way through something. Junior doctors? Pretended they knew how to work a blood pressure cuff. Senior nurses? Definitely had a moment of standing in a cupboard, wondering what they walked in there for. The trick isn't knowing everything—it's knowing when to confidently pretend you do, then quietly figure it out before anyone catches on. And if all else fails, there's always the universal backup plan: furrow the brow, exhale thoughtfully, and say, "Hmm, let's double-check that." Works every time.

Chapter 13: Scrubs, Sneakers, and Tattoos – The Ward's New Fashion Rules

Right, so you're on the ward, doing your best to remember which end of the thermometer is the business end, and it hits you: nurses are fashion icons now. Gone are the days of starched white uniforms that make you look like you're auditioning for *Casualty*. The modern nurse is a whole mood, strutting around in uniforms that might be more 'comfy chic' than 'clinical clean,' and let's be real, half of the hospital now feels like an impromptu runway show.

But before we get carried away, let's talk about the wardrobe basics first:

tunics. Oh, the tunics! NHS uniforms aren't scrubs in the American sense—no, no, we don't have that glam. What we get are these tunics, often in a range of unflattering shades that make you look like you belong in a school cafeteria. Remember when you were a student nurse, and you tried to get the size right? You'd squeeze into a size 10 and wonder why it felt like a straitjacket, then swiftly jump to a size 16 because your arms couldn't even bend, and suddenly you were swimming in fabric. Ah, the struggle for the right fit. There's no easy way out. But you do what you have to. You go up a size, just to make sure you can move without the risk of turning blue from lack of circulation. Besides, it's not like you're on a catwalk—more like a hospital ward where no one's checking the fit of your tunic.

But then, as the years go by, things change. The world is waking up, and so is the NHS. You start to see nurses who *actually* look like themselves. *People with personality*. The days of hiding tattoos are over. What was once the hidden ink under sleeves is now on display in full force—no longer tucked away for fear of a formal warning. You'll find sleeves, necks, and wrists covered in detailed tattoos that are nothing short of artistic masterpieces. And hey, why not? If you're spending 12-hour shifts in a hospital, you might as well wear your artwork proudly. Plus, as long as you're not using your tattoos to diagnose anything, there's not much to complain about.

Facial piercings are another thing. You'd never have seen a nurse with a nose stud in the good ol' days. Oh, how things have changed! You'd be met with raised eyebrows if you dared to wear anything more than a stud in your ear. But now? Nose studs, eyebrow piercings, and even the odd cheek piercing are no longer the rebellious statements they once were. You'll even find nurses flaunting *multiple* piercings like it's no big deal. People can be a bit judgmental, sure, but you've probably got an entire playlist of "I'm doing my best" playing in your head as you work through the shift. And who can argue with that? You're saving lives, not just slinging meds, and anyone who questions your style probably needs to focus on the patient rather than the piercing.

And then, there are the shoes. Oof, let's talk about the shoes. Remember the days of those horrible, clunky, hospital-issued clogs that could give you blisters just by *looking* at them?

Those were dark times. Now, though, every nurse seems to be rocking a pair of shoes that *look* like they've just stepped out of a high-end sportswear catalogue. Seriously, you've got Nikes, Sketchers, and even fancy running shoes making an appearance on the ward, like we're all training for a marathon in between rounds. It's a revolution, people! Gone are the days of dodging puddles of disinfectant while praying your feet don't fall off after a 12-hour shift. Nurses need comfort, and they've figured out that a pair of supportive trainers beats a pair of ugly plastic shoes any day.

But let's not forget the important, yet often-overlooked, weapon in the student nurse's wardrobe: *smelly shoe spray*. When you're in your first year and still working out the logistics of being on your feet for the whole day, that spray is your best friend. If only they sold it in bulk. There's nothing like the sweet smell of lavender or lemon to cover up the scent of a day's worth of feet crammed into poorly ventilated shoes. Honestly, it should be a part of the NHS induction process, right alongside hand hygiene training.

Now, you've done your best to make it through the shift looking like a well-functioning human being. You've got your comfy shoes, your tattoo-adorned arms, and your carefully-hidden necklace. Yes, we've all tried to make those subtle style choices under our tunics. I mean, there's only so much you can do with a hospital-issued outfit, but a cheeky bit of pale pink nail polish peeking out from under your gloves, or that gold necklace you've hidden just enough so no one notices—these are the little things that keep you going. Because, let's face it, when you're staring down the barrel of another 12-hour shift, sometimes a little sparkle or pop of colour is all that's needed to keep you sane. But beware of that one senior nurse, who has a sixth sense for uniform violations—like a bloodhound on the scent of non-regulation attire. If they catch sight of even a sponge of paint, they'll materialise out of thin air, armed with a bottle of industrial-strength acetone that strips not just the polish but also a layer of dignity, and the skin on your fingers, leaving your fingertips a ghostly shade of hospital-grade white. Although, in all fairness, the last thing you would want as a patient is the dropping of nail varnish all over your wound that is being dressed, maybe the manager has a point after all.

And don't even get me started on hair. Once upon a time, nurses were all about the sensible bun. Now, nurses are experimenting with rainbow-coloured hair, tight curls, braids that could have come straight off Pinterest, or occasionally, something so straight and sleek it looks like it's been ironed in place. Honestly, the nurses' hair game is as diverse as the patients' needs. So long as it's out of your face, right? We all know how disastrous it is when someone's hair ends up in a wound dressing.

In the end, nursing uniforms have come a long way. They've evolved to reflect not only the demands of the job but also the personalities and identities of the people doing the job. Sure, it's still about comfort and practicality—but there's no harm in making it look good while you're at it. So whether you're sporting a nose stud, a sleeve of tattoos, the most comfortable trainers you can find, or even a cheeky hidden necklace, just remember: you're still saving lives. And, really, if anyone questions that, they're just jealous of your style. or just a stickler for the rules, how dare they cramp our style.

Chapter 14: The NHS Family – Claps, Cheers, and A Lot of Waiting Around

There's something special about the healthcare team. We might be overworked, underpaid, and always on the brink of a breakdown, but we come together when it counts. And nothing sums up the NHS like that pointless clap for the NHS during COVID. Remember when we were all standing on our doorsteps, clapping for the brave souls working in healthcare? It lasted about five minutes, but for those of us in the trenches, that clap felt more like a giant slap on the back. The NHS workers are literally holding the system together with tape, coffee, and sheer willpower, and a clap felt a little... underwhelming, right? Nothing like a clap from the safety of your own home to raise the spirits of a healthcare worker in the trenches pumping on the chest of a critically ill patient whilst humming the classic Staying Alive theme tune like it is Saturday night in 1978.

But that said, despite the applause, we stand together. In the face of chaos, there's nothing like the team spirit between nurses, doctors, support staff, and even the cleaning crew. We're all in this together, battling the same issues, supporting each other, and, frankly, complaining about the lack of toilet paper in the staff bathrooms and the same water tap that's been broken for centuries. We might not always agree on the best way to care for a patient, but one thing's for sure: We've got each other's backs. or in the case of the student nurse, where you're stuck in the great in-between, not quite a member of the team, nor a member of the public. Stuck where it's deemed unprofessional to make friends with qualified staff, even after you have spent the day being their personal errand boy. Perhaps it's the backwards way of remaining professional? Or maybe it's to keep you on your toes. An invite to any morale-boosting events is way out of sight until you are deemed worthy of the team, or when you get your pin, sucks right? Well, nursing students have their crew, the more relatable ones, their fellow students, also being shunned from any kind of relationship bonding with their new co-workers. And often, you even find you make friends with the newly qualified nurses who find themselves in a strange place, and they are actually being spoken to. But after three years of silence, they have reduced themselves to living the life of a hermit crab, learning to stay quiet in the back so they find comfort in talking to people who are familiar with what they know.

Chapter 15: The Final Stretch – The 12-Week Gauntlet

Ah, the final stretch. The last 12 weeks of your nursing journey. You've survived years of lectures, placements, exams, and that one time you thought "Just one more chapter" at 3 a.m. when you should've been sleeping. But now, here you are. It's like the marathon of all marathons, except instead of running, you're juggling exams, placement assessments, competency sign-offs, and desperately trying to avoid looking like you've just stepped out of a wind tunnel after attempting to apply foundation in the dark.

You can't quite tell if you're more exhausted than excited. It's like when you're on the last leg of a giant jigsaw puzzle and there's that one elusive piece missing. You've checked under the couch, behind the TV, even inside the dog's bed (don't ask how), and you're beginning to wonder if the piece was just never meant to be. You're *so* close to the end, but you're also overwhelmed by the pressure to nail every skill, every task, and make it look like you've got it together, even if you're secretly Googling how to tie a bandage before the shift starts. The dream job seems just within reach, but so is the nightmare of being placed on a ward where your mentor's idea of a challenge is bandaging a limb while blindfolded.

And let's not forget the job applications. Oh, the job applications.

The endless parade of CVs and cover letters. You send one off, then another, then a third. Each time, you pray that somewhere out there, someone—anyone—will see the gem that you are and offer you a job that doesn't involve 12-hour shifts, excessive paperwork, or the endless battle with blood pressure cuffs you can never seem to find. And, of course, there's always that voice in your head asking: *Am I ready? Am I going to make it through this?*

But it's not just the looming job hunt that's on your mind. No, no. It's the terrifying, soul-crushing experience of trying to get all your competencies signed off. Oh, you thought you could coast to the finish line? Think again. You've got a massive checklist of skills you need to demonstrate, ranging from the glamorous (like taking blood pressure) to the terrifying (like catheter insertion—please don't let me mess this up, oh God). And yes, somehow, you've left half of them to the last possible minute. Why? Who knows. Maybe it's the adrenaline, maybe it's just the sheer inability to deal with pressure, but suddenly, the pile of paperwork seems like a mountain you didn't see coming. Every skill is listed, waiting to be ticked off by a mentor who may or may not be paying attention. They might be sitting there, signing off "drug administration" without even looking up from their phone. Or they might ask you to demonstrate a skill *for the fifth time* while making you feel like you've been in this exact situation since the dawn of time.

Now, let's talk about the next big hurdle: getting your skills signed off by a qualified nurse. Here's the fun part: they don't just sign off on your competencies; they also have to put their NMC nursing PIN in your book to confirm they're happy with your skills. And if they sign it off and you mess up, they're essentially putting their professional reputation on the line. It's a big deal because, in a way, they're signing away their own accountability. So, when you're standing there, waiting for them to sign that little box, you can practically feel the pressure.

You might notice that, on occasion, the nurse you're asking to sign you off looks slightly more anxious than you'd expect. They might even ask, "Are you sure you're confident with this? Because once I sign this, I'm putting my name on it." And it's true—they're basically putting their NMC PIN on the line for you. It's not just a casual signature. That PIN represents their professional identity, and by signing off on you, they're vouching for your abilities. So, don't be too offended if they ask you a few more questions or double-check your technique. They're doing their due diligence, and they're responsible for you—whether they like it or not.

If they're hesitating or looking a bit unsure, don't take it personally. It's not that they don't believe in you—it's more like the "this is a big deal" realisation dawning on them, too. Keep your cool, stay humble, and answer questions confidently. You don't want them feeling like they're signing off on something they might regret later. You're in this together, and the last thing you want is a mentor nervously crossing out their signature because you weren't prepared.

So, when that moment finally comes and your mentor signs off that they're happy with your skills, complete with their NMC PIN, it's a huge deal. You've earned it, and they're putting their faith in you to do it right. Don't forget to thank them for that responsibility, because they're not just handing you a "Done" sticker—they're vouching for your future as a nurse.

Now, let's talk about working as a nurse's assistant. If you're not careful, the last 12 weeks can feel like you're in a perpetual state of "shadowing." You're learning, yes, but also doing a *lot* of the grunt work. You're the person grabbing supplies, cleaning up, making tea, fetching a spoon when someone wants one, trying to look professional while basically being an unpaid assistant. But hey, it's part of the deal, right? The key to surviving this? Show as much interest as humanly possible. Ask questions, even if you think you already know the answer. Nurses love someone who's genuinely eager. Just avoid the urge to be cocky, even if you feel like you've mastered every step in the nursing textbook. You're not a seasoned pro yet—no matter how many bloods you have taken. If you get too full of yourself, someone will remind you of how long it took you to master the art of putting on gloves without them ripping.

The key advice I can give. Never stop learning, even when you feel like you've *done it all.* The truth about nursing is that no matter how far you've come, there's always another thing to learn. So, when you're in those last few weeks, don't look at the clock or count the days until you can finally collapse into your bed (though let's be real, that bed looks like the promised land). Keep your head down, keep learning, and keep asking questions. Because once you get to that finish line, you'll realise—no matter how much you've struggled along the way—that it's all been worth it. And when you sign that competency sheet (finally!), the weight of the world will seem a little lighter.

And if you mess up? Well, let's just say that if you fail to meet your competencies, you might find yourself stuck repeating the last 12 weeks… basically working for free again. But don't worry about that now. Just take a deep breath, stay focused, and remember: nursing is a marathon, not a sprint—so pace yourself and leave the *running* to the athletes. You've got this.

Chapter 16: The Final Shift – Knuckling down, it's getting real

There comes a time, usually after about six months of late-night study sessions, endless patient care plans, and more caffeine than should be humanly possible, when you finally get to have the big moment: your final shift. It's the moment you've been waiting for. You step into the ward, tunic on, ready to go. And then you get hit with the realisation that, yes, you're finally doing this for real. No more pretending, no more "student nurse" title, no more hanging around hoping that someone will come to the rescue when a situation gets too intense. It's *you* now. You're the one people will look to for help.

But even in that moment, there's a small voice in the back of your head that says, "Are you sure? Should I call someone? What if I mess this up?!" And that voice? It's the voice of every single nurse who has ever stepped into those shoes. It's the voice of self-doubt and imposter syndrome that will always be there, lurking. But here's the kicker—*everyone* feels it. Even the seasoned veterans. By now, you've learned one very important lesson: nursing isn't about knowing everything. It's about knowing where to find the answers, being willing to ask questions, and not being afraid to say, "I don't know, but I'll find out for you."

You've got the skills, the knowledge, and the ability to learn. And that's what makes you a real nurse. Not the badge or the title or the fancy new uniform. It's the heart, the drive, and the desire to keep going, even when you're sleep-deprived, on the 12th hour of your shift, and have a patient asking about their medication for the fifth time. It's about caring, genuinely caring for others—even when your body is telling you it's time to curl up into a ball and take a nap for three days straight.

But this is why you do it. This is why you're here. Nursing isn't just about the medicine, the procedures, the vitals and assessments—it's about the people. It's about making a difference, however small, in someone's life. It's about being there when someone is at their most vulnerable and helping them feel a little more comfortable, a little more human.

And maybe, just maybe, it's about making sure your patients don't have to hear *too many* jokes about "the wonders of the human body" while you try to lighten the mood during a particularly tense moment. (Although, let's be honest, some of them do laugh. Eventually.)

Epilogue: A Day in the Life – Always a Nurse, But Never Quite Ready

So, you've made it. You've finally graduated, you've got the badge, and you're officially a nurse now. You can practically hear the confetti falling as you step onto the ward for your first shift as a qualified nurse. You walk in with that gleam in your eye, ready to take on the world—or at least the one patient who insists their IV is too tight and needs immediate adjustment for the third time in an hour. You think, that's it, I'm a qualified nurse. I can work by myself now. Time to show the world my new skills!

Hold up. What's this? Supernumerary?

Wait, what? You thought the days of supernumerary (aka, "the extra pair of hands that don't really count") were behind you, didn't you? Well, guess what? Now that you're officially a nurse, you're working alongside another nurse—because apparently, the NHS doesn't want to risk you going it alone just yet. You may have years of training under your belt, but nope, you're still being babysat, and it's honestly like being back in the student days… minus the uniform that feels like it was designed by a sadistic fashion committee.

Oh, and let's not forget: supernumerary isn't guaranteed for long. Because of staffing. You know how it is in the NHS. One minute, you're happily shadowing a colleague, getting a feel for the chaos of the ward, and the next minute, you're thrown into the deep end with no extra hands. Staffing shortages don't care if you are just qualified or if it's your first shift. You might have a few weeks- maybe even months- of this "*I'm here to learn from you*" experience. However, don't get too comfortable. You never know when your supernumerary status could be slashed faster than a nurse can swipe their card at the vending machine.

And while we're at it, the skills workbooks—remember those? The ones you thought you'd waved goodbye to after you handed in your final placement portfolio. Yeah, they're back. Just when you thought you were free from endless checklists and worksheets, you now have the 'completed skill assessments' haunting you like an uninvited ghost at a Halloween party. You thought they were behind you, but oh no. There's more! Now you're checking off wound care, IV starts, and drip rates with the same enthusiasm you had for the 17th multiple-choice test back in your first year.

And let's not forget that new reality: being a nurse means you're never quite ready. Even when you think you've nailed a skill, the job throws something new your way. You'll get used to the early mornings, the 12-hour shifts, and somehow always have a half-eaten sandwich lying around at 4 p.m. because you're too tired to finish it. You might even *accidentally* eat it at 11 p.m. When your brain can no longer distinguish between "hunger" and "pure survival mode".

But here's the kicker: even after all of this, you're still in it for the right reasons. You wanted to make a difference, to be the one who's there when it counts the most, to be the person they call at 3 a.m. when the world is falling apart and they need a steady hand to help put it back together. Sure, it's a mess. It's tough. It's exhausting. But it's also the most rewarding thing you'll ever do.

So, to all the future nurses out there—you've made it through this book, but more importantly, you're going to make it through the wards. The long hours, the endless paperwork, the crazy patients, and the days when you find yourself sobbing in a toilet stall (remember, we've all been there)—that's just part of the journey.

And in the end? You're more than just a nurse. You're the lifeline someone else is holding onto when everything else falls apart. And that's a damn big deal. Now, grab a coffee (or a ten-minute break to inhale some stale sandwich crumbs), change into your tunics, and get ready for the next shift. The journey? It's only just begun.

The End (or is it?)

Thank you for joining me on this wild ride of student nurse life. Maybe you've laughed, maybe you've cried, and you've probably googled things you never thought you would. But at the end of it all, one thing's for sure—you're ready. You've got this.

So here's to you, the nurses of tomorrow, Take it one day at a time. And remember, even when the going gets tough, there's always a cup of coffee, a quiet moment, and a future full of endless possibilities ahead. And to the people who came along for the ride out of pure curiosity. I hope this has given you a real insight into student nurses today. Thank you.

Want more real talk, rants, and ridiculous nurse stories?

Join my Chaos Crew for exclusive free content, sneak peeks of new books, and things they definitely didn't teach us in training.

Scan below or visit:

https://linktr.ee/vitalvoicepress

PS: Loved the book? Leaving a review is like clapping for the NHS… but actually helpful.

References:

Royal College of Nursing (RCN) (2024) RCN student survey: Nursing students and the impact of workforce pressures. Available at: https://www.theguardian.com/society/article/2024/jul/03/half-of-nursing-students-in-england-have-considered-quitting-survey-finds (Accessed: 25 March 2025).

Royal College of Nursing (RCN) (2024) *New nurse numbers collapsing in every English region as RCN warns 10-Year Plan at risk*. Available at: https://www.rcn.org.uk/news-and-events/Press-Releases/New-nurse-numbers-collapsing-in-every-English-region-as-RCN-warns-10-Year-Plan-at-risk (Accessed: 25 March 2025).

Silva, D.A.S., Petroski, E.L., Gaya, A.C.A. and De Oliveira, I.O. (2019) 'Weight gain and associated factors among nursing students: A longitudinal study', BMC Nursing, 18(1), pp. 1-10. Available at: https://pmc.ncbi.nlm.nih.gov/articles/PMC6781428/ (Accessed: 25 March 2025)

Siddique, H. (2018) 'Quarter of UK student nurses drop out before graduation, study finds', The Guardian, 3 September. Available at: https://www.theguardian.com/society/2018/sep/03/quarter-of-uk-student-nurses-drop-out-before-graduation-study-finds (Accessed: 25 March 2025).